Piano • Vocal • Guitar

Contemporary Latin Songs

W9-BXA-496

ISBN 0-7935-1576-9

Hal Leonard Publishing Corporation
7777 West Bluemound Road P.O. Box 13819 Milwaukee, WI 53213

Copyright © 1993 by HAL LEONARD PUBLISHING CORPORATION
International Copyright Secured   All Rights Reserved

For all works contained herein:
Unauthorized copying, arranging, adapting, recording or public performance is an infringement of copyright.
Infringers are liable under the law.

AMIGOS PARA SIEMPRE
(FRIENDS FOR LIFE)
(The Official Theme of the Barcelona 1992 Games)

Music by ANDREW LLOYD WEBBER
Lyrics by DON BLACK

© Copyright 1992 The Really Useful Group Limited, London
All rights for North America controlled by Williamson Music Co.
International Copyright Secured   All Rights Reserved

life not just a sum-mer or a spring A - MI - GOS PA - RA SIEM - PRE._____

AMOR ETERNO
(EL MÁS TRISTE RECUERDO)

Words and Music by
JUAN GABRIEL

Copyright © 1984 BMG ARABELLA MEXICO, S.A.
Administered in the U.S.A. by BMG Songs, Inc.
International Copyright Secured   All Rights Reserved

Tú   e - res   la   tris - te - za   ay   de   mis
Yo   he   su - fri - do   tan - to   por

o - jos.
tu   ausencia.

Que   llo - ran ____   en   si - len - cio ____   por   tu   a -
Des - de   ese ____   dí - a   has - ta   hoy   no   soy   fe -

12

ANGEL BABY
(Angelito Mio)

Words and Music by
ROSE HAMLIN

It's just _ like heav - en
D.S. Nun - ca _ me de - jes _

be - in' here _ with you. _
so - la y _ sin ti; _

You're like _ an an - gel, _
que sin _ tu a - mor _ no

too good _ to be true. _
quie - ro vi - vir. _

But af - ter all _ I
Por - que _ te quie - ro, _ te

© 1960 (Renewed) by Windswept Pacific Entertainment Co. d/b/a Longitude Music Co.
International Copyright Secured   All Rights Reserved

love you I do. _____ An - gel ba - by, __ my an - gel ba - by. __
quie - ro en - se - rio... An - gel mi - o, __ mi an - gel - i - to. __

When you __ are near me __ my heart skips __ a beat, __
It's just __ like heav - en __ here with __ you dear, __

I can hard - ly stand __ on __ my own __ two feet, __
I can nev - er stay a - way __ with - out __ you near, __

To Coda ⊕

be - cause __ I love you __ I love you, I do. _____ An - gel ba - by, __
be - cause __ I love you __ I love you, I do. _____ An - gel ba - by, __

BARROCO

By BEBU SILVETTI

© 1987 BEBU MUSIC PUBLISHING
All Rights Controlled and Administered by EMI APRIL MUSIC INC.
All Rights Reserved International Copyright Secured Used by Permission

BELLA SEÑORA (BELLA SIGNORA)

Lyrics by L. DALLA
Music by M. MALAVASI

Copyright © 1989 MIMO EDIZIONI MUSICALI S.r.l. and EDIZIONI DAMALUMA S.r.l.
Administered in the U.S.A. by BMG Songs, Inc. and S.I.A.E.
International Copyright Secured   All Rights Reserved

28

CON TU AMOR

Words and Music by
JUAN GABRIEL

Copyright © 1986 BMG ARABELLA MEXICO, S.A.
Administered in the U.S.A. by BMG Songs, Inc.
International Copyright Secured   All Rights Reserved

a ol - vi - dar, _ ol - vi - dar, _ ol - vi - dar _ el do - lor. _____

Con tu a - mor ____ se fue - ron mis pe -

- nas. Y lle - gó ____

la fe - li - ci - dad. ____ Gra - cias a tí __

no sien - to tris - te - za, _____ ni do - lor_

so - lo soy fe - liz.___

Pe - ro con tu a -

mor   se fue - ron mis pe - nas._____

CORACAO APAIXONADO

By FERNANDO ADOUR
and RICARDO MAGNO

© 1985 EMI SONGS HOLLAND B.V. / B.V. POP SONGS ROTTERDAM
All Rights for the U.S.A. Controlled and Administered by EMI APRIL MUSIC INC.
All Rights Reserved   International Copyright Secured   Used by Permission

COSAS DEL AMOR

Words and Music by ROBERTO LIVI
and RUDY PEREZ

Copyright © 1991 LIVI MUSIC and JKMC MUSIC PUBLISHING, INC.
International Copyright Secured All Rights Reserved

41

DULCE MIEL

By CLAUDIO RABELLO,
RENATO CORREA and CHRISTINA LARRAURA

Quie-ro es-tar jun-to a tí

ju - gar jun-to a tí   te - ner li - ber - tad

© 1990 EMI SONGS DO BRAZIL LTDA. and SONY SONGS DO BRAZIL LTDA.
All Rights for EMI SONGS DO BRAZIL LTDA. Controlled and Administered by EMI APRIL MUSIC INC.
All Rights Reserved International Copyright Secured Used By Permission

ESTOY SENTADO AQUI

By CESAR ROSAS

Es - toy ___ sen - ta - do a - qui,

que me pa - sen la te - qui - la, el a - mor y tris - te vi - da no me im - por - ta a

© 1988 Ceros Music (BMI)
Administered by Bug Music
International Copyright Secured   All Rights Reserved

50

HASTA QUE TE CONOCI

Words and Music by
JUAN GABRIEL

No sa - bí - a ___ de tris - te - zas ni de lá - gri - mas ni na - da que me hi -
ví - a ___ tan dis - tin - to; al-go her-mo-so al-go-di - vi - no, lle - no

cie - ran llo - rar. Yo sa - bí - a ___ de ca - ri - ño, de ter -
de fe - li - ci - dad. Yo sa - bí - a ___ de a-le-grí - as, la be -

nu - ra, ___ por-que a-mí ___ des-de pe - que - ño ___ e - so me en-se - ñó ma má;
lle - za y ___ de la vi - da, pe - ro no de so - le - dad;

Copyright © 1986 BMG Arabella Mexico, S.A.
Administered in the U.S. by BMG Songs Inc. (ASCAP)
International Copyright Secured All Rights Reserved

54

HEY

By JULIO IGLESIAS, G. BELFIORE,
M. BALDUCCI and RAMON ARCUSA

Hey

no va - yas pre - su - mien - do por a -
no cre - as que te ha - ces un fa -
re - cuer - do que ga - na - bas siem - pre
a - ho - ra que ya to - do ter - mi -

© 1980 SUNNY POP SONGS B.V. / EMI SONGS HOLLAND B.V.
All Rights for the U.S.A. Controlled and Administered by EMI APRIL MUSIC INC.
All Rights Reserved   International Copyright Secured   Used by Permission

sé que a tí te gus - ta pre - su - mir   de -
ve - ces que es me - jor que - rer a - sí   que
sé si tú tam - bién re - cor - da - ás   que
cre - as que te guar - do al - gún ren - cor   es

cir a los a - mi - gos que sin tí   ya no pue - do vi -
ser que - ri - do y no po - der sen - tir   lo que sien - to por
siem - pre que in - ten - ta ba ha - cer la paz   yo era un rí o en tu
siem - pre más fe - liz quien más a - mó   y e se siem - pre fuí

vir.
tí.
mar.
yo.   Ya

LA FUERZA DE AMAR

Words and Music by RONALDO BASTOS
and CLEBERSON HORSTH

Copyright © 1991 BMG ARABELLA LTD. and TRES PONTAS EDICIONES MUSICAL LTDA.
Rights of BMG ARABELLA LTD. Administered in the U.S.A. by BMG Songs, Inc.
All Rights for TRES PONTAS EDICIONES MUSICAL LTDA. Controlled and Administered by EMI APRIL MUSIC INC.
International Copyright Secured   All Rights Reserved   Used by Permission

LA PISTOLA Y EL CORAZÓN

By DAVID HIDALGO
and LOUIE PEREZ

© 1988 Davince Music/No K.O. Music (BMI)
Administered by BUG MUSIC
International Copyright Secured All Rights Reserved

con la pis - to - la y el co - ra - zón.

LLORANDO SE FUE (LA LAMBADA)

By ULISES HERMOSA
and GONZALO HERMOSA

© 1986 PROMOCIONES Y EDICIONES INTERNACIONALES, S.A.
All Rights for the World Excluding Mexico Controlled and Administered by EMI APRIL MUSIC INC. and SONY TUNES INC.
All Rights Reserved   International Copyright Secured   Used By Permission

MARE

Words and Music by ALDO RUBEN A. YANCE, RONALD J. ORTEGA,
JOSE LUIS P. PACHO and ENRIQUE M. ARELLANO

Copyright © 1991 BMG ARABELLA MEXICO, S.A.
Administered in the U.S.A. by BMG Songs, Inc.
International Copyright Secured   All Rights Reserved

78

(Spoken:) Hace cuatro meses que salí de Yucatán y me vine en camión a la ciudad.   Vine a visitar a unos parientes, que
(Spoken:) Una mañana me invitaron a pasear. Fui a Chapultepec, la latino y coyoacan. Mis parientes resultaron muy decentes

viven aca por insurgentes.   Mu-chas   ni - ñas   lin-das. Mu-cha   tan-ta vio-len-cia.
y esa noche decidí irme a reventar. Mu-cha   luz en la ca - lle. To - do   es des-par-pa-jado

(Spoken:) Mucho ruido y mucha gente.   Yo mejor me regreso a Yucatán.   Me   regreso   a   Yuca -
(Spoken:) La verdad yo prefiero los xipiles. Y mejor me regreso a Yucatán.

tán.   Me   regreso   a   Yuca - tán.

80

MALA SUERTE

By BEBU SILVETTI
and ROBERTO LIVI

© 1989 BEBU MUSIC PUBLISHING and LIVI MUSIC
All Rights for BEBU MUSIC PUBLISHING Controlled and Administered by EMI APRIL MUSIC INC.
All Rights Reserved   International Copyright Secured   Used by Permission

MIS AMORES

By BEBU SILVETTI
and ROBERTO LIVI

Los a -

© 1989 BEBU MUSIC PUBLISHING and LIVI MUSIC
All Rights for BEBU MUSIC PUBLISHING Controlled and Administered by EMI APRIL MUSIC INC.
All Rights Reserved   International Copyright Secured   Used by Permission

89

POR ELLA

By JULIO IGLESIAS,
RAMON ARCUSA and MANUEL DE LA CALVA

© 1980 EMI SONGS HOLLAND B.V. / SUNNY POP SONGS B.V.
All Rights for the U.S.A. Controlled and Administered by EMI APRIL MUSIC INC.
All Rights Reserved   International Copyright Secured   Used by Permission

G7

sé sin es - pe - rar - lo de don Juan a con - quis - ta - do fue
vi - da en blan - co y ne - gro se vis - tió en co - lo - res neu - vos fue } por
bié tan - to de pron - to y me e - na - mo - ré del to - do fue
to - dos se pre - gun - tan por quién can - to mi a - mar - gu - ra es

Cmaj7   1,3 A7♭9   2,4 Gm7   C7

el - la.___   Por   Por

Fmaj7

el - la.___   { Sé que me mue - ro por
                                                     { Tan - tos «Te quie - ros» por

Cmaj7

el - la ___ ～   { to - do lo he si - do } por
el - la ___ ～   { tan - tos re - cuer - dos }

QUIERO AMANECER CON ALGUIEN

By DANIELA ROMO
and BEBU SILVETTI

© 1989 BEECHWOOD DE MEXICO S.A. and BEBU MUSIC PUBLISHING
All Rights for BEBU MUSIC PUBLISHING in the U.S.A. and Canada Controlled and Administered by EMI APRIL MUSIC INC.
All Rights for BEECHWOOD DE MEXICO S.A. in the U.S.A. and Canada Controlled and Administered by COLGEMS-EMI MUSIC INC.
All Rights Reserved International Copyright Secured Used by Permission

TODO, TODO, TODO

By JOARSACI

© 1990 EMI MUSICAL, S.A. DE C.V.
All Rights Controlled and Administered by EMI APRIL MUSIC INC.
All Rights Reserved International Copyright Secured Used by Permission

mal. Crees que es-tás en tu de-re-cho pe-ro te has e-qui-vo-ca - do __ y un día de tan-tos me de-

ci - do y __ te pon-go en tu lu - gar. Úl - ti - ma -

men - te que es-tá pa - san - do. No tie - nes tiem - po o no has que - ri -

- do. No es-tés pen - san - do que es-to es un jue - go y ten en
men - te. *(Instrumental)* No tien - es

VEN Y DAME UN POCO MÁS

By BEBU SILVETTI
and SYLVIA IBANEZ

can-do un a - mor sin - ce - ro tu ve a ven - tu - ras que no re-cuer-
ve - ces yo me cre - í - a que e - ra to - das a - quel que - rí -

© 1989 BEBU MUSIC PUBLISHING and LIVI MUSIC
All Rights for BEBU MUSIC PUBLISHING Controlled and Administered by EMI APRIL MUSIC INC.
All Rights Reserved   International Copyright Secured   Used by Permission

Y VOY A SER FELIZ

Words and Music by
XAVIER SANTOS CORTEZ

ho- ra es- tás___ que te vas ___ y si te vas, pues ve-

Copyright © 1984 BMG-EDIM, S.A. de C.V.
Administered in the U.S.A. by BMG Songs, Inc.
International Copyright Secured   All Rights Reserved

YOU DON'T HAVE TO GO HOME TONIGHT (ESTA NOCHE)

Words and Music by DIANA VILLEGAS,
SYLVIA VILLEGAS, VICKY VILLEGAS,
ERIC LOWEN and DAN NAVARRO

Copyright © 1991 Sony Songs, Inc., Salsongs, Marion Place Music,
Careers-BMG Publishing, Inc., Famous Music and Tres Hermanas Music
Rights for Sony Songs, Inc. and Salsongs Administered by Sony Music Publishing, 8 Music Square West, Nashville, TN 37203
All Rights on behalf of Marion Place Music Administered by Career-BMG Music Publishing, Inc.
International Copyright Secured All Rights Reserved

116

26 CONTEMPORARY HITS

An assortment of today's favorite hits, including: Achy Breaky Heart • Baby Baby • Beauty And The Beast • Make It Happen • Save The Best For Last • Tears In Heaven • This Used To Be My Playground • Where Does My Heart Beat Now • and many more.
00311599 $12.95

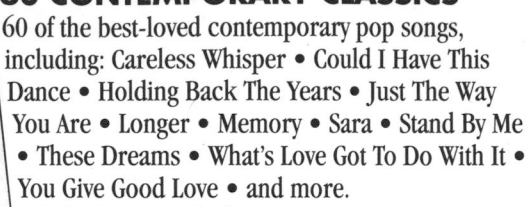

Contemporary
CLASSICS
LIGHT HITS FROM YESTERDAY & TODAY! ARRANGED FOR PIANO, VOICE & GUITAR

EASY LISTENING STANDARDS

75 classic and contemporary favorites, including: Chances Are • Edelweiss • Endless Love • A Foggy Day • Just The Way You Are • Misty • My Way • People • Somewhere Out There • Strangers In The Night • and many more.
00311504 $14.95

60 CONTEMPORARY CLASSICS

60 of the best-loved contemporary pop songs, including: Careless Whisper • Could I Have This Dance • Holding Back The Years • Just The Way You Are • Longer • Memory • Sara • Stand By Me • These Dreams • What's Love Got To Do With It • You Give Good Love • and more.
00361078 $16.95

66 CONTEMPORARY STANDARDS

66 contemporary classics, including: All Around The World • Black Velvet • Candle In The Wind • Careless Whisper • Every Breath You Take • Every Rose Has Its Thorn • Here And Now • Hold On • How Am I Supposed To Live Without You • I Wanna Be Rich • Imagine • Kokomo • Memory • Red, Red Wine • Sacrifice • Time After Time • We Didn't Start The Fire • What's Love Got To Do With It? • You Needed Me • and more.
00490501 $16.95

THE ADULT CONTEMPORARY SONGBOOK

48 of today's best light hits, including: Candle In The Wind • Don't Know Much • Every Breath You Take • How Can We Be Lovers • Love Takes Time • Sacrifice • Somewhere Out There • Vision Of Love • and many more.
00311529 $15.95

CONTEMPORARY BALLADS

58 favorite ballads, including: Can't Smile Without You • Careless Whisper • Endless Love • Green Green Grass Of Home • Just The Way You Are • Let It Be • Longer • Love On The Rocks • My Way • Same Old Lang Syne • Sometimes When We Touch • Time After Time • Yesterday • You Needed Me • more.
00359492 $16.95

CONTEMPORARY LOVE & WEDDING SONGS

26 songs of romance, including: Can't Help Falling In Love • Could I Have This Dance • Endless Love • I.O.U. • Just The Way You Are • Longer • Somewhere Out There • Sunrise, Sunset • You Needed Me • Your Song.
00359498 $10.95

THE NEW GRAMMY AWARDS SONG OF THE YEAR SONGBOOK

An updated edition that features every song named Grammy Awards "Song of the Year" from 1958-1988. 28 songs, featuring: Volare • Moon River • The Shadow Of Your Smile • Up, Up And Away • Bridge Over Troubled Water • You've Got A Friend • Killing Me Softly With His Song • The Way We Were • You Light Up My Life • Evergreen • Sailing • Bette Davis Eyes • We Are The World • That's What Friends Are For • Somewhere Out There • Don't Worry, Be Happy.
00359932 $12.95

NEW AGE PIANO SAMPLER

11 new age selections by Yanni, John Jarvis, Suzanne Ciani, Jim Chappell and Eddie Jobson. Includes biographies and photos of each featured artist. Pieces include: Velocity Of Love • After The Sunrise • Homecoming • and more.
00360690 $10.95

RHYTHM & BLUES BALLADS

34 wonderful ballads by some of the best R&B artists—Earth, Wind & Fire, Gregory Abbott, Luther Vandross, Angela Bofill, and Gladys Knight & The Pips. Songs include: Careless Whisper • Earth Angel • Just Once • Sara Smile • Sexual Healing • Shake You Down • and more.
00360870 $12.95

SOFT ROCK-REVISED

40 romantic mellow hits, including: And So It Goes • Beauty And The Beast • Don't Know Much • Save The Best For Last • Tears In Heaven • Vision Of Love • Your Song • and more.
00311596 $14.95

TIMELESS HITS

32 pop standards, including: Copacabana • Could I Have This Dance • Fire And Rain • Green Green Grass Of Home • I.O.U. • Longer • Piano Man • Stand By Me • We're In This Love Together • What A Wonderful World • You Are My Lady.
00490095 $12.95

For more information, see your local music dealer, or write to:
Hal Leonard Publishing Corporation
P.O. Box 13819 Milwaukee, Wisconsin 53213

Prices, contents, and availability subject to change without notice.